CW01081739

Also by Cynthia Fuller

Moving Towards Light (Flambard Press, 1992)
Instructions for the Desert (Flambard Press, 1996)
Only a Small Boat (Flambard Press, 2001)
Jack's Letters Home (Flambard Press, 2006)
Background Music (Flambard Press, 2009)

estuary

Poems

CYNTHIA FULLER

RED SQUIRREL PRESS

First published in the UK in 2015 by
Red Squirrel Press
Briery Hill Cottage
Stannngton
Morpeth
Northumberland
NE61 6ES
www.redsquirrelpress.com

Red Squirrel Press is distributed by Central Books Ltd.
and represented by Inpress Ltd.
www.inpressbooks.co.uk

Designed and typeset by Gerry Cambridge
gerry.cambridge@btinternet.com

A CIP catalogue record for this publication is available from the
British Library.

ISBN: 978 1 910437 06 3

Printed in the UK by Martins the Printers Ltd
on acid-free paper sourced from mills with FSC chain of
custody certification.
www.martins-the-printers.com

Contents

In memory of my parents

HARRY (1906–1967) & DOROTHY (1907–1975)

Estuary

salt marshes drowning, dissolving, lost
in brown water
       the pools drained away
silt settling, turning back
into land
       neither dry land nor water

cliffs cracked underfoot, fractured
       tumbling
grassy boulders like ruins
       littering the shore
and the waves crashing higher
       pulling them, breaking them
laying them down—
       neither water nor land

the island kept moving as if trying
       to fit the fray of its coastline
       to the edge of the mainland,
to escape from the beat of the sea

       but we faced the other way
out to the estuary
where the tide meets the river—
where the streams and marshes
were haunted
       by owlers and wreckers
       and ghosts from the plague ships

our water was brackish, our sandbanks uncertain
no solid ground   nothing is constant
when land turns to water
                    fresh water to salt

Island Girl

Water defined us. We were *Island Girls*
prone to be late when the bridge ratcheted up
to let through a pulp boat on its way to the mill,
holding back our train packed with eleven plus passes.

Island Girls—top pupils of the Island's Primaries—
who soon discovered we weren't so special among
the daughters of farmers, doctors, solicitors—
in Co-op uniforms, pushing against the tide.

The sea defined us. We biked down Seaside Avenue,
swam in The Aquarena, bought chips at the Jetty Café,
our streets were Marine Parade and Neptune Terrace,
Sunday night dances at the Seaview, our Ritz.

But one night looking out across the estuary I saw
the mainland lights were mocking—the Island's
groynes and quicksand were trying to contain me,
holding me back behind deep water channels.

I packed up my schooldays, the fairground, the boyfriends,
tucked the sighing of shingle deep under my books.
I gave up the Island as the bridge let me pass.
I headed northward and inland away from the coast.

The Isle of Sheppey, January 31st 1953

Sea walls were breached that night, wooden shacks
battered and swollen. Boats turned to matchwood,
breakwaters to sponge in their cover of slime.

Way out in deep water long-legged fortresses
would not protect us, wobbled towards us
on rusty stalks, pushed to and fro by the waves.

Buoys bobbed faster around the sunken warship,
its masts signalling a crooked warning,
the cargo enough to blow us sky high.

The sand had always been dangerous, sucking
at legs, at the clattering cockleboats
that risked the low tide, erasing all marks.

We understood our edges would be eaten away,
a house on the cliff top becoming
a scatter of bricks on the beach below.
dissolving us into the estuary's silt.

We had lived with the slow gnaw of erosion,
but after that night we would watch the horizon
for the sudden storm massing,

for the wall of salt water that would swamp fields,
drown sheep, wash away our limits,
dissolving us into the estuary's silt.

Place of Birth

1

If place can be a ghost, you're haunting me
as if to pull me back, or punish me for
leaving early and wanting to forget.

You come back in a patchy way, a map
with parts wiped out, as if a mug of tea
had stood there, or sunlight faded out the print.

Some streets are clear, the buildings as they were
but then they stop—bleached out—and I can't find
the sea front path beyond the Jetty Café.

I learnt early to distrust your sand spits.
They looked so solid as the tide went out
but one step and they would suck a body in.

Your marshes were the same—colour, the key.
The brightest green must be jumped over
or wellies would stick fast then start to sink.

Is it like that, this haunting, a tug back
to the unsafe ground—estuary silt,
mud flats, the threat of no firm footing.

2

Leaving seemed so easy then, no tears,
nothing too heavy to carry as I would
be back. I wanted to cross your bridge,

to go where no one knew whose daughter
I was, to put together the pieces,
the bolshie girl, the wild girl, the clever.

We left, heads full of plans and no idea
that tragedies would bring us back, parents
faltering instead of staying as they were:

hospital visits where they became children
in their tight-tucked sheets, seeking reassurance
from children who pretended to be grown up;

funerals, where we dressed the part and poured the tea
to hide the panic, aware only of the way
the day was gaping wide with absence.

This time, I take everything with me.
Home is a pocketful of keepsakes.
No place. I won't be coming back.

3

But half a lifetime on you interrupt,
breaking in with fragments—a glimpse of lane,
a corner shop, the prefabs, the canal.

Not even snapshots, more the torn pieces
from an old album, the blown bits left
after a bonfire, scattering across my view.

There's no point, I don't remember, but
then I start filling in gaps—Love Lane,
Houston's sweet shop and one stretch of road

that's never gone—sea lapping on my left.
It's always dusk. I'm on my bike, pedalling
hard to get a good speed up, pushing against

the dynamo's pull to make my front light
burn away the shadows as I pass
the beached catamarans, to make the welcome
whirr shut out the muffled clink, the jingle.

It never worked. Each time I was dizzy with fear
at the way the masts were moving in still air.

4

More cycled road—this time it's Barton's Hill—
the last house before rough ground—and faces
from the edges, the very borders

of remembering – the Bennett sisters.
Three, long-legged, short-skirted, moving in
a jangle of bangles, earrings swinging;

black gypsy eyes and hair heaped to tumble
over proud shoulders—like exotic birds
in bright plumage, they would silence the bus queue.

They towered over their squat mother (called *witch*
for her burning stare) and over the fourth sister,
Barbara, with her heavy woman's body,

a girl's bow in her hacked hair. Her tactic
was speed, her voice a roar of rage as she
hurtled down the path, and into the road

to seize my handlebars, wrench me to a stop
with her strongman's arms. She would lean into
my face, her laugh hot with triumph and threat.

But why these random places, these faces
from the periphery—as if memory
once shed a light too bright

on the main players, fading them, leaving
only obscure edges, shadowy corners.
And why always fear? That girl could be

high on dreams, dancing a tightrope
in a sparkly circus outfit.
She didn't need your tacky fairground

rides to feel alive—struts all banged back
together to be shaken apart each time—
her helter-skelter days were risky but

her grip was sure. She balanced danger
with knowing when to jump.
You bring me back a girl pedalling

into the wind. The real fear was how fierce—
how absolute—was the urge to work up speed,
to rattle her old bike across the bridge,

to leave.

Nurture

Did it start there,
with the woman crying
among the packing cases,
the small girl stilled, the baby
turning in her darkness.

Or was it later,
with the sudden departures,
her coat gone from the peg,
the suitcase missing,
silence left behind.

Like threading a needle,
we learnt to read
her restlessness.
The house was not home
to her but exile.

We breathed her desire
for escape, set shallow
roots like her, lived out
her wish to swim
beyond the breakwaters.

Halfway Road

How often you dream these pavements
dusty with summer. Are you small
that the view is this close up?
A sudden lizard flicking
into life, hot baked stillness
reanimating—so quick
that you might have blinked it.

This route between sweet shop and home
is fixed in a perpetual
August afternoon. How you want
to see the girl but the angle
gives only the path, her toes
grubby in worn-out sandals,
the verge she is scouring for toads.

Rags and Bone

My mother was the only one I knew
who'd been inside, shushing the barking dogs,
finding a way through the pipes and cogs,
the stacks of newspaper, sacks of old clothes.
Not really a house—one part Nissen hut,
the other, railway carriage without wheels.
An eyesore, said the neighbours—but to children
a draw, despite the dogs and fierce cockerel.

There was a man once, wizened and quick,
dusty in a black suit, eyes that flicked away.
Now just the small mother and her daughter
who towered over her, a moon face blank,
tinged oily yellow. She didn't speak.
The mother pushed a cart around our streets,
wiry frame flexed against the weight,
collecting all the things we didn't want.

We would dare each other to brave the dogs,
knock on the door, look in, but picturing
the stolid daughter mute in her outsize
gabardine, the mother searching through
our discarded things, subdued us—
that, and my mother's certain rebuke,
as I knew she always greeted them from
the silence of the bus queue.

Crossbar

Emotions budded then like tender breasts,
her child's certainty giving way to doubt.
Her chatter became shy, all the 11 plus
cleverness failed. Not yet 13 she was hatched
but not steady. On the cusp. He took her up,
an older boy, set her on his crossbar.
She could not learn her body's new behaviour—
why whispers in her hair brought tears near,
the brush of a bare arm made her shiver,
hands warm through the damp of her swimsuit
melted her belly, like fear.
As if she were still the child she couldn't be,
he dropped her for an older girl. Heartbreak
was easy to learn, that first grown-up hurt.

Pegman

There is nothing now like freewheeling in the dark
down Breakneck Hill, dynamo whirring, heart dancing
with the danger, eyes scanning the flying bushes
for the man that might be waiting, might lunge out to
snatch you from your speeding Hercules bicycle.
You'd read about the man in secret in Sunday
papers, knew you could be prey, not understanding
all the details, only wondering if he might
be like the Pegman with his stretched out neck and head,
his rough red skin and flapping mac with too short sleeves,
who couldn't speak, just uttered sawing sounds as if
his throat was rusty. Your mother said that he was
harmless and you never let on how he loomed up
from behind a breakwater in the dusk and how
you ran and ran but couldn't tell because you weren't
allowed on the beach so late and they might have stopped
your whirling bike rides through the dark as punishment.

Wall of Death

She stood looking down from the rim on to
engines thundering, sparking, breathed in
the lethal heat of oil, scorch of rubber;
the whole structure resounding, vibrating.

She was fifteen. In the speed of her travelling
she just managed to keep hold of the driver's
cold leather jacket; scarcely able to get off
the bike, her legs so numb and stiff as if

they didn't belong to her, as if
she'd slipped out of her own body
somewhere back along the road, halfway
between the parents who didn't want her

to ride pillion, and the driver
who brought her to this barrel of danger,
this ramshackle construction, to watch
how only speed kept the bikes up there,
kept them circling, circling the wall.

Soundscape

Theme tunes, catch phrases, Billy Cotton,
Mrs Dale, *Workers' Playtime, Round the Horn*
laying down complex strata of sound:
Saturday teatime was hushed for
the metrical reading of match results;
Sunday lunch tensions ratcheted up by
the tender greetings of *Family Favourites.*
Harry Carpenter disrupted my homework.
I left for the bus with *Lift Up Your Hearts.*

But my geology could not settle
the unscheduled voices—a fault line
under the house at night. Stripped
bare in the darkness, they had no cover
of programmed noise, no Home Service
restraint—raw words distorted by anger.
I had nowhere to lay down their pain.

Callers

At the time she didn't understand
why the red light above the porch
had led the drunk Swedish sailor
to their door, had misled him
all the way up their muddy hill
in the darkness to ring and ring
at the bell, rousing their father
who said there were no girls there,
set him right, sent him on his way.

But she put that lost sailor
with the other man who hammered
on their back door one Saturday
when she was alone, who asked where
her parents were, asked for water,
and afterwards she locked the door—
even the stiff bolts—and leaned
against it, shutting out his wild face,
his thirst, the boots that didn't fit.

Home Game

She could not get used to the transformation—
her mild father shouting in a new voice,
a raging stranger waving his glasses
at the linesman, roaring surprising abuse.
On the smoky top deck of the homeward bus
her quick glance would check he was changing back,
shutting himself down until the next match.

Years on, she came to welcome that stranger,
when the World Cup revived him, brought him out
from his tunnel of silence. How she teased—
his scorn for *the new-fangled boots like slippers,*
his rage at *foreigners' fashion for diving.*
They railed at the ref's blind spot, the offside
striker, passing banter between them, a team.

My Father in the Sixties

Indoors, 1960

He opens the sitting room door
where my mother is entertaining.

He has forgotten the visitors
he refused to see. He's just heard

something interesting on the Home Service.
He stands with the door half open,

leans into the new hush, talking.
He wears the usual jumper—

matted lovat, his baggy old trousers.
A cigarette burns away in his hand.

When he's told them, he closes the door,
withdraws to his kitchen, his wireless,

his fortress of silence breached only
by these sudden and random desires to report.

My mother will break the sitting room
silence. She is practised, word perfect.

In the Garden, 1962

He is kneeling on an island,
a beret on his head, snipping.

The grass is waist high, steps and paths
are lost in the wilderness.

He is enclosed in the steady murmur
of John Arlott from his transistor.

He works the shears with a regular
rhythm, pausing to shift to a new spot,

to throw away his butt, to light up.
The grass stretches far, his islands are small.

One day when the grass is cut, he will
tackle the overgrown beds, the orchard

shoulder-deep in nettles, the derelict garage
where the rats are breeding. Meanwhile

there is a refuge in slow snipping,
in the soft sounds of cricket.

My Mother and the Viscount

In a cabin of sleeping passengers,
ear drums bursting as we drop,
as the pilots radio
that two engines aren't firing,
as we fall through the deepest dark,
I do not wake my fellow traveller.
With the night plunging past
I have no more to say to him.

Instead, I think how my mother has
kept faith with life, remember
the walking stick she would hook over
the rear bar of my tricycle
to hold back my rides into danger.
Alone among sleepers,
though the dark is seductive
I surrender the plane to her care.

Passenger

Once she had locked her fear in a box
which he could not open,

once she had remembered the trick
of making her eyes say nothing,

he had to ratchet up the game, increase
the stakes to try to make her stay.

She fell into the trap, agreed to be taken
to the station one last time. He drove

a long way round—to the road that traversed
the dual carriageway. Stopped.

Cross your fingers, he said and put his foot
down. The van jumped, sped forward

across the southbound lanes. Stopped.
And again. She closed her eyes, waited

for the metal walls to crunch in on her,
jamming them together for always.

Then they were over—his familiar hands
still on the wheel—his white fixed face.

She climbed out of the danger,
took her bags, didn't look back.

After the Honeymoon, 1937

The new husband pours from the frosted jug—
the art deco set, their honeymoon treat,
a touch of chic from a Paris boulevard.
He passes his wife the glass inscribed *Toi*,
keeping *Moi* for himself, plain tumblers
for his new parents-in-law. They are stiff—
uneasy guests in the modest home.
No one mentions how they sent her away
but the room crackles with it—the months,
the homesick hours she wandered to prove
their love; the letters—his heart wide open
in brave italics. Now he sets the jug down,
turns it so the words are facing them,
gold script outfacing them: *Nous Deux*. Nous Deux.

Revenant

In dreams you mingle
with the living, inhabiting
your old live self, convincing—
almost—that not a single
moment should be lost in grieving.

Asleep, a part of me is hopeful—
how much I want to believe,
to breathe in deep relief;
a part is wary, mistrustful,
remembering that well of grief.

Waking, I turn in time—almost—
to see you cross back over.
You leave behind a tremor
in the air, shadows and dust,
empty space becoming emptier.

Upperthorpe

She is looking for herself in old photos—
years of selected moments, preserved
with neat edges. She is nowhere there.

But they stir up others—drowned images,
the moments not chosen—the sprigged cotton
of the dress her mother sent as a surprise

that summer—how the short straight skirt
won't let her be quick when she needs to run
up the endless steps. Her legs will not work.

How they are heavy like legs that will not run
in a nightmare, but this is real—
June sunshine is bright in this stranger's garden

whose steps she must climb as fast as she can
with her lungs bursting and no breath left
to ask for help, to ask someone to phone

for help. The image, which she cannot hold,
slips out of focus, but she knows that girl,
a mother until that afternoon

when a shutter came down
and cut her off
from the days before and all she had been.

Exile

The girl has forgotten how to be ordinary,
how to brush past others in the crowd,
how to nod or smile, at home there.

She cannot cross into the sunshine.
She can only traverse the winter field,
her feet unprotected, her heart

pushed up into her throat.
A secret is embedded in her chest.
It has forced a passage

through her ribs and settles
into the cavity at her centre,
making her bones give way.

She dreams of stopping a stranger,
voicing the words that wedge
her tongue against her teeth.

How can it be she was a girl once
who thought the dancing days
would last forever in her red tapshoes?

Charm Bracelet

Her hands were not like my mother's.
Sharp bones at knuckle and wrist
threatened to poke through.

A heavy charm bracelet jangled
and clattered. I wanted her
to sit and show me each charm,
tell me each story, but she was

a flurry of laughter
between table and aga
in her farmhouse kitchen, between

henhouse and orchard, her red hair
wild. Thin as a whip, angular,
skin scattered with freckles,
she didn't sit down.

When they lost the farm, she was
cooped in a town flat, shut up
far from fields, worn out
with no jobs to do.

Farmer's daughter, farmer's wife,
she was stilled by misery,
her bony hands useless in her lap.

The Soloist

As he loses his way in the Beethoven concerto
the music begins to unravel around him,
the orchestra splitting—flute, clarinet, viola.
The notes and patterns are in the tips of his fingers
but tonight life is sneaking in between the chords.
The air shifts, players are lowering their instruments,
uneasy whispers and murmurs flit round the hall.

He sits on in the ruin of the concerto—
the notes are all tangled, cadenzas scattered.
Arpeggios are rippling with accusations,
the left hand melody is a breaking heart.
From major to minor—she loves him, she left him.
A long diminuendo, no final crescendo,
he sits on at the piano. There will be no applause.

A Norfolk Carpenter's First Angel

At first he didn't trust their talk—
travelling carpenters fresh from London,
full of success and too much ale.

They boasted of angels fine carved in oak,
set high in a roof's arched ribs—
angels taller than a man, wings spread.

Drawn in, he questioned them—position,
dimensions, breadth of timber.
He tested their words—*hammer beam, spandrel.*

For days he watched the master carver,
noted each cut, each groove, stored
safe in memory every line and turn.

He chose the piece of oak that called to him,
sensing the way the body lay
waiting in the wood to be released.

As if thawing from deep cold his fingers stirred.
He began to see an angel's face,
his shape, his hands held up in peace.

St Cuthbert on Inner Farne

How the small boat rode the swell
  tossed like flotsam
    steadied by prayer

a cloud of curious fulmars
  circling calling

He left the shared bread
  the community
    of compline

for the kittiwake colony
  the turmoil of terns

choosing solitude among sea birds
  the salt lash of the storm
    inhospitable hermitage

sea cresting and crashing
  sending spray swirling

no silence in the buffeting wind
  but the silence within
    stillness gathered

divine contemplation
  among puffins and eiders

How his spirit grew strong
  icy shallows his abbey
    the night sky his dome

Hide

We click up the wooden flaps, perch and wait.
The flaps themselves, the wobbly bench, even the door
hold greater interest for a three year old
than the still water with its mirrored sky.
We gaze out; scan the surface for a glimpse.
Two coots meander, a group of distant ducks
push on farther. We shush the voices, the feet
that fidget, the rocking of the bench.
Keep still! You'll frighten everything off.
As if in answer, a ring disrupts the loch,
just yards away dark head pops up—
slick arc of body—tail. All disappear
to reappear closer, rippling, twisting,
disturbing the water's sheen. Still closer,
absorbed in play, the otter is untroubled
by our boys. Now part of his hide and seek,
eyes skim the water—*There! No, there. See!*—
until it's time to let down the flaps
and clatter out. We grown-ups carry home the way
the neat head broke the surface in reproof.

Still

In the lee of the hill a man is waiting,
the brown of his jacket lost in the hawthorn's
winter tones. His dogs—one white, one black—
stand sharp against the muddy bank. He holds
them on a short leash, close against his thighs.
Their thin coats do not disguise the tremor,
the way acute attention shivers through them.
Nothing moves. There is no wind. They wait.
Under hedges, in ditches, small creatures
know to keep still. Only their senses quiver,
they listen, sniff the air. The loosed dogs
will speed to kill the rabbit, or the cold field
will send the man home, pockets empty—
one slip, one murmur, will break the spell.

Baiting

Two otters sleep in drowsy coils, the third
tunnels inside the woman's shirt
like a shifting bosom as she describes
their needs and habits, their rescue.

These are safe, named and cherished in
their Cotswold home. Their rescuers come north
to Weardale's annual country show,
spreading the word about fur coats and cruelty.

A man in camouflage from neck to boots
slips through the crowd like a weasel.
He holds two fell hounds on a tight leash,
begins to whistle through his teeth.

The dogs are nervy. Alert at once,
the otters are drawn to the wire,
to the insistent sibilance.
He shows his dogs—*Otters. See!*

He scorns the classy Southern voices,
the care for creatures best left wild.
The Cotswold couple can only watch,
their eccentricity no match for menace.

By Myself

Because the bus is late we are sudden companions,
the man at the bus stop and me. *I've seen you before,* he says,
You're always by yourself. I smile. *You don't go down
the club. Don't you drink? I don't drink now. Not much.*
He is standing just too close. *I don't remember anything.*
He's bulky, head shaven, eyes grey and empty,
disconnected from his smile. He has no teeth. He frowns,
Have you got a husband? Because a husband would be
useful to this exchange, I begin to create one.
I expect he's at work, is he? He'll drive. I dream him a job
where he travels, commutes in his bright blue Ford.
The man is nodding now, as if he can see him.
Because there is a husband, he can relax.
My Mam's ninety now and failing. It's sad to see people fail.
A ghost of misery passes over his features.
When we get off the bus together, he heads for
the Day Centre. I turn to say goodbye but he looks blank.
Will he remember anything of me, or the necessary husband.

Moorbank

Take refuge here. The garden is
a cup of breathing green
rimmed by the city's noise—
the swell and drone of cars,
the lost dogs barking to go home.
It is a living habitat
for urban birds—a nest of song.
Roots are pushing deep below
concrete and tarmac.
Time could slow here to the pace
of ancient trees, or quicken
to keep step with the sudden poppy
whose orange tissue flares
and crumples in a day.

The Greenhouse

She slides the door closed, her world is ordered,
the temperature is even: trays line up
in rows, her labels name and sort them.

Her careful fingers prick out seedlings,
pot them on, move them up the ranks,
settle each in its proper place.

She moves between benches, attentive
to the bud near to bursting, the twist of a leaf,
she tests for moisture, alert to disease.

The rattle of the generator—
its regular rhythm—has become hers,
sealing her in, letting her be.

At five she will slide the door open
to the roar of the city's disorder
returning her to her own—

but for now she is gardener,
for now the plants hold her; she breathes
their humidity, absorbed in their growth.

Physic

These old people are sick with winter.
See how cold has eroded their bones.
They are wheeled in with tubes trailing,
uprooted from their homes.

Take them out into the garden
where spring is beginning to break through.
Start slowly with the yellows of narcissus,
forsythia and primrose—a pale warmth.

Let them touch the green of leaves unfurling
to ease the knots and clutches of their joints.
Only then, you might risk the tulip's startling scarlet
transfusing colour to parched skin.

When they are stronger, wheel them to the hothouse.
Let the delicate mouths of orchids surprise them
into memories of forgotten loves.
Settle them gently. Let them doze and dream.

How to Care for a Garden

Sit still in the garden until the birds forget you.
Their warning chinks and whirrs will settle into song.

Set your feet firm on the earth.
Seeds and bulbs have found nurture here.

Breathe the thrill of clean air.
Let the green travel through your veins.

Sit still in the garden until your skin
could be leaf, your fingers twigs.

Now you will understand sunshine
and all the vagaries of rain.

This is growing—and you are so still
that the birds no longer see you.

They peck for sustenance at your feet.

Waiting Room

It hurts to breathe.
A hand is squeezing
his heart.

He spreads his own hand,
soil still rimming
his nails—

he was setting seed
in careful rows,
she danced in,

kissed him, *Won't be late*
danced out—
his fingers shake.

Someone will come,
a stiff uniform,
a prepared face.

It hurts to breathe.
In a space between days
he waits.

If someone asked
he would say she is
a flower

for him—winter
aconite, the year's
first bloom,

too bright for this
white place, too full
of hope.

He wants
to take her home.

By Way of Silence

She sits straight-backed, hands stilled.
Day drains out of the kitchen,
chrysanthemums on the table glow
with the last of it. She listens.

She knows the silence is a thin skin
over the sounds she wants to hear,
its surface can be puckered, broken.
Once—unless she dreamt it—she heard

footsteps' certain progress down the lane,
the familiar change of pitch as they reached
the yard. Then silence claimed them.
She knows she must not will it.

She must wait. But she cannot stop
her mind seeing the hand reach
for the latch, lift it; the door swing
inwards; then his figure at the threshold.

She cannot stop her mind and his face is
so pale, his mouth a bruised berry,
his eyes smudged stars. How taut
his body is, braced against her longing.

Teatime

He scuffs his shoes against the table
willing them to tell him off.
He cannot trouble the silence.

Even before he takes a mouthful
he feels the lump like pebbles
gathering in his throat.

Sometimes at school he forgets.
Each time, remembering
is like falling, all breath lost

in the lurching drop and he must
punch himself hard, hurt himself,
must punish that forgetting.

If he dares, he thinks of before.
Teatime was jokes and stories,
teasing and laughing, all together.

Four now three and it is always winter.
How safe it was to be the younger son.
'Only' has no one to keep off the cold.

The Catch

At the end of the pier darkness washes up,
swallowing the man in oilskins and cap.
Afternoon has crept into evening.

He does not move. The sea laps against
the wall, a gentle rolling rhythm; no wind.
His catch is meagre—two mackerel
already dulling, to be gutted later.

He sits on when he should pack his tackle,
move, go home. His joints have settled into
pain, his shoulders hunch with its weight.

He sees the gate, the path, the front door,
his key in the lock, the darkened hall,
his wife in her chair, the stove unlit;
how sorrow has turned home comfortless.

Post War Wedding

The pain of the last years
hollowed him out—

the elder son lost in France,
his wife' slow drift from him,

her grieving eating
heart and breath from her.

As if he could turn back
time's leaden hands,

he went back to find her,
the landlady's daughter

who had a smile for him
thirty years before.

A forgotten belonging,
the love frozen in her,

hope a pale memory
when he came back for her.

Stiff in her spinster dress
she made her vows,

as if she could
fill the empty chair,

dispel the chill for him,
settle the restless ghosts,

and cherish the silent son
who refused to call her mother.

The Lesson of Water

Before she was five
she learnt about water.

From the top of the hill she saw
the silver snake of the river

had swallowed the fields in the night,
making them lakes

where sky and clouds floated.
The sheep were changed into

grey sodden sacks caught
under hedges, bobbing in ditches

when they should have been grazing
where there should have been grass.

She learnt that the sea had not stayed
in its place, had crashed over the wall,

broken through cracks, so down in the town
streets were changed into rivers

and people rowed boats and waited
upstairs as the sea pushed them out.

The pictures stayed in her head.
She grew up wary of water.

It could not be trusted
to stay between banks, behind walls.

Even a quiet sea could be waiting
to turn, to sweep them away,

dump them stranded and swollen
like those heaps of drowned sheep.

Visiting the Estuary

When you walk across wet sand, look behind you,
  your footprints are pooling, soon there's no trace.

Try to run and sand turns mud, tugs at your feet, sucks you down
  where cockles are blowing their tell-tale bubbles.

Temporary sandbank, low water refuge—
  watch out for the tide's turn, the drowned sea bed.

Lick your salty fingers—when did river become sea—
  brown Thames meeting grey ocean, mixing waters.

Watch your step—sediment—mudflat —salt marsh—
  where are the boundaries—no firm footing—

You are not welcome among the pools and marram—
  silt shifting, edges eroding. Go back where you came.

Groundwork

1

Uncovering the Borders

She is weeding her mother's garden again,
clearing the front beds where the scarlet poppies
used to flaunt their sooty hearts.
She is trying to remember how her mother
set the borders out, but all the time
behind the house she feels the wilderness
creep closer. She works slowly
on hands and knees, searching through
memories to find the plan, the layout,
the instructions that she needs.

As day fades the house looms up,
its terracotta tiles darken to deep red.
It does not call her, with its closed doors,
its twisting stairs. Too many ghosts.
Someone has nailed the windows shut
to keep them in. She is unsure
where to sleep safe: her mother's room
has emptied out all trace of her.
There are always intruders waiting to slip in.
The flower beds will be work enough for now.

2

Not at Home

If she went inside she might meet the girl
who woke alone and found the house
had grown bigger, swollen with night;
and the boards along the passage rattled
and shifted where the huge industrial
hoover had sucked out the tacks
that kept it all steady. Even the blue
glow of the Aladdin stove, and its sleepy
warm smell, couldn't make her feel safe.
The passage was longer; there were
too many doors. Once she reached
the room where her father should be
sleeping, she knew before she looked
that he wouldn't be there. Only
the two of them, and he wouldn't be there.

3

A Menagerie of Souls

If she went inside, she might become keeper
for the restless souls of all the lost creatures:
the field mice which nested in the rusty stove;
the decapitated rats laid to rest
among dusters deep in scullery drawers;
the bird intruders layered in chimneys,
all bones and feathers and the sweet smell of rot;
the generations of lean tabbies,
their cardboard box litters and daily kill,
and in the kitchen the ghost of a horse
shifting from hoof to patient hoof
on the quarry tiles, head in a nosebag.
She might gather around her this motley flock,
to keep at bay the other lonely ghosts
for whose misery she has made no plan.

4

Giving her Away

As it is, she tries not to look back
to the doorway where shapes keep forming
and breaking. She knows who they are but wills
them away. She doesn't want to remember.
She is the one who knows the bride is lying.
Her father is giving her a chance to escape,
opening the door on a flowery meadow.
But she is trapped by deceitful sequins
on her dress, white blossom in her hair.
Only she knows the bride is a fake,
just a frightened girl in satin slippers,
with a baby curled safe inside her—
no one to save her from the wilderness.
She must concentrate on weeding, leaving
father and daughter fading on the steps.

5

The Ghosts are Insistent

Soon darkness will blot out the borders
and paths—but the ghosts are distracting.
She feels them behind her, pressed to the glass.
They whisper their stories. They want something
from her. She could wrench out the nails,
throw open the windows, let them all go—
the lodgers, the grandparents, subletting
tenants, renegade horse thieves would
come tumbling out. But what of her parents?
Which version—her father the suitor,
her mother the teacher, or the troubled
reclaimers of wrecked house and garden?
She hopes they'll be sober with plans
and instructions, not high on the glamour
of dance shoes and turquoise shantung.

6

Her Mother in Wind and Fire

Her mother is disappearing round the corner
in a gust of wind. A headscarf blows
behind her like a pennant. She is clutching
the Dyno rods, making for the orchard,
the septic tank, the blockage. Her mother's
small frame bristles with intent, excitement,
as she is bowled along like tumbleweed,
laughing at the energy the wind releases.
She will scatter rats, cats and strangers
who sneak in to plunder her violets.
She'll have stashed away the can of paraffin
in the corner of the ruined outhouse,
ready to splash it liberally to waken
one of her many bonfires—her blue
conflagrations of sky-dancing flames.

7

Her Father Enchanted

And there goes her father. He has left
all the jobs he will never get finished.
His shoulders are defeated. He is on his way
shopping in his seen-better-days coat,
with the weekly cheque that spells out failure—

only to reappear leading a horse
(a small horse for he is a small man)
with woven saddle cloth, loose rope bridle.
Her gaucho father wears a broad brimmed hat,
orange poncho and fine flared bombachas.

He clicks to his horse, springs on its back,
sets off to the shop down the unmade road.
He is singing in Spanish, a man
who knows no languages, and has never,
to her knowledge, ridden a horse.

8

After her Parents Left Home

Without them the house is beginning
to shrink. Its terracotta façade
is patchworked with blanks where tiles are missing,
and birds are flying in through the gaps.
Paint peels. The sign he made swings crooked.
Inside, poplar roots are lifting the floor,
pushing door frames out of kilter. Cracks spread
their tendrils across the walls. In corners
all the other ghosts are huddled
with no power to stop the wilderness.

Like a wise parent she watched them go
their wayward ways. They left no instructions,
no plan for her to follow. She can
pack up her tools, close the gate behind her.
She remembers a picture book—
a castle all overgrown with briars,
roses blooming and tumbling over the roof.
Let these poppies grow tall, these peonies swell,
let wallflowers riot, honeysuckle clamber
till the house is hidden, safe from intruders.

Acknowledgements

Some of the poems have appeared
in the following publications:

'Island Girl', *Friction*, 2010; 'Pegman' *Gift:
A Chapbook for Seamus Heaney* (NCLA, 2009); 'My Father
in the Sixties'; 'Teatime', *The North*, Issue 49, 2012; 'After
the Honeymoon, 1937', *ARTEMISpoetry,* Issue 9, 2012;
'Revenant', *The Book of Love and Loss* (ed. R.V.Bailey and
June Hall, 2014); 'The Soloist', *ARTEMISpoetry,* Issue
12, 2014; 'St Cuthbert on Inner Farne', *Shadow Script: 12
poems for Lindisfarne and Bamburgh* ed. Colette Bryce
(NCLA 2013); 'Moorbank'; 'The Greenhouse'; *In the Poet's
Garden—Anthology* http://everywherewaseden.wordpress.
com/anthology/; 'Waiting Room', *Under the Radar,* Issue
Eleven, 2013; 'By Way of Silence', *Other Poetry,* Series Four,
Number Seven, 2012.

With thanks to Sheila Wakefield, Founder-Editor at Red
Squirrel Press, Linda France, Jackie Litherland, Newcastle
Women's Poetry Group, and Tess Spencer.